Mastering 11+

Maths
Numerical Reasoning
Practice Book 2

First Edition

ashkraft
EDUCATIONAL

Mastering 11+ © 2016 ashkraft educational

This page is intentionally left blank

Mastering 11+
Maths / Numerical Reasoning
Practice Book 2

First Edition

Copyright © 2016 ASHKRAFT EDUCATIONAL

ISBN-13: 978-1910678213

ISBN 9781910678213

9 781910 678213

Imprint ID: 20162304/1

DEDICATION

All the little mathematicians practicing for the
Eleven plus challenge.

"It's not that I am so smart;
it's just that I stay with problems longer."

Albert Einstein

Table of Contents

SHORT MATHS

EXERCISE 1: Short Numerical Reasoning

Instructions: Work out and select ONE correct answer for each of the questions.
Mark your answer on the answer sheet. *Maximum time allowed: 10 minutes*

1 A block of cheese weighs 4.34 kg. It is cut into seven equal pieces.
What is the weight of each piece, in grams?

A	B	C	D	E	F
6.2 g	0.62 kg	6.2 kg	62 g	620 kg	620 g

2 What is the total of all internal angles of an equilateral triangle?

A	B	C	D	E	F
60°	30°	90°	180°	120°	40°

3 What is 75% of £4200?

A	B	C	D	E	F
£315	£1300	£3150	£3100	£3000	£1980

4 What is **0.25 x 150**?

A	B	C	D	E	F
37.50	37.05	3.75	375.0	34.5	37.15

5 Though how many degrees does the **hour hand** of a clock turn in 60 minutes?

A	B	C	D	E	F
15°	30°	40°	45°	60°	90°

6	How many times does 0.25 go into 175?					
	A	B	C	D	E	F
	70	47	700	57	7	17

7	What is 10% of 10^3?					
	A	B	C	D	E	F
	10	100	1	1000	103	10.3

8	Workout $-3 - 3$					
	A	B	C	D	E	F
	0	6	-6	3	-3	1

9	What is the remainder when you divide $3^2 + 4^2$ by 7?					
	A	B	C	D	E	F
	9	25	1	2	3	4

10	What is $\frac{2}{5}$ of 1000?					
	A	B	C	D	E	F
	400	2500	40	160	250	25

11	What is $\frac{13}{20}$ as a percentage?					
	A	B	C	D	E	F
	7%	6.5%	70%	65%	13.5%	15.3%

12	What is the product of 0.5 and 0.5?					
	A	B	C	D	E	F
	0.025	0.25	2.5	25	5	1

13 Which of the following is the smallest?

A	B	C	D	E	F
0.6	6%	¾	½	¼	$\frac{13}{20}$

14 How many Vertices does a cube have?

A	B	C	D	E	F
2	4	8	12	14	6

15 What is the perimeter of a regular Octagon whose side is 0.3cm?

A	B	C	D	E	F
18	1.8	15	1.5	2.4	24

Answer Sheet:

1	A	B	C	D	E	F
2	A	B	C	D	E	F
3	A	B	C	D	E	F
4	A	B	C	D	E	F
5	A	B	C	D	E	F
6	A	B	C	D	E	F
7	A	B	C	D	E	F
8	A	B	C	D	E	F
9	A	B	C	D	E	F
10	A	B	C	D	E	F
11	A	B	C	D	E	F
12	A	B	C	D	E	F
13	A	B	C	D	E	F
14	A	B	C	D	E	F
15	A	B	C	D	E	F

EXERCISE 2: Short Numerical Reasoning

Instructions: Work out and select ONE correct answer for each of the questions.
Mark your answer on the answer sheet.   *Maximum time allowed: 10 minutes*

1

Here is an equation: $5n = 20$

What is the value of **12n?**

A	B	C	D	E	F
4	36	48	60	72	84

2

Find the value of angle "m".

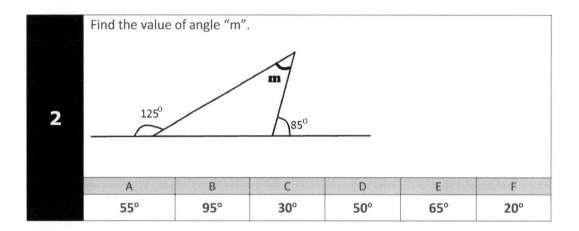

A	B	C	D	E	F
55°	95°	30°	50°	65°	20°

3

Here is a sequence.

24   36   48   60   72

Which of the below represent the sequence?

A	B	C	D	E	F
4n+1	2n+2	12 + n	12(n+1)	12n+1	6(n+1)

4

There is a bag that contains 2 red balls and 3 white balls. What is the probability of pulling out a white ball as a percentage?

A	B	C	D	E	F
2%	12%	20%	5%	1%	10%

5	What is $30 - (25 \div 5) + 7$?					
	A	B	C	D	E	F
	8	42	6	7	32	22

6	Which of the following equations gives the largest value, when **n** is 5?					
	A	B	C	D	E	F
	2n	n^2	n+1	(n+1)/n	2n – n	3n+1

7	Find the area of the triangle.					
	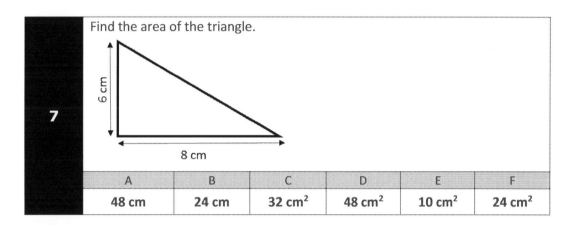					
	A	B	C	D	E	F
	48 cm	24 cm	32 cm^2	48 cm^2	10 cm^2	24 cm^2

8	A party hall calculates cost of hosting a birthday party using the formula below. **Cost = £9.00 x number of children + £50** What is the cost of party for 12 children?					
	A	B	C	D	E	F
	£96	£108	£158	£148	£136	£129

9	A train from Liverpool leaves at 6:55 PM and arrives and Colchester Town at 8:15 PM. How long is the journey?					
	A	B	C	D	E	F
	1 hr 15 min	1 hr 20 min	55 min	1 hr 10 min	2 hr 5 min	2 hr 20 min

10	Tickets to a play costs £5.50 for an adult and £2.50 for a child. What is the total cost if a couple took their three children to see the play?					
	A	B	C	D	E	F
	£18.50	£17.50	£16.50	£16	£17	£18

11 — The length of the rectangle is twice as long as the height.

The perimeter is 18 cm. What is the area of the rectangle?

	A	B	C	D	E	F
	18 cm²	9cm²	12 cm²	22 cm²	38 cm²	21 cm²

12	The price of a dining table is £560 and is on sale at 25% discount. What is the discount amount on offer?					
	A	B	C	D	E	F
	£420	£520	£120	£140	£125	£145

13	What is the maximum individual angle of a right angled triangle?					
	A	B	C	D	E	F
	45°	60°	75°	90°	55°	35°

14	What is 3^3+9^2 ?					
	A	B	C	D	E	F
	108	27	56	71	101	110

15	What is the product of 0.3 and 0.15?					
	A	B	C	D	E	F
	0.45	0.045	4.5	4.51	0.18	0.315

Answer Sheet:

1	A	B	C	D	E	F
2	A	B	C	D	E	F
3	A	B	C	D	E	F
4	A	B	C	D	E	F
5	A	B	C	D	E	F
6	A	B	C	D	E	F
7	A	B	C	D	E	F
8	A	B	C	D	E	F
9	A	B	C	D	E	F
10	A	B	C	D	E	F
11	A	B	C	D	E	F
12	A	B	C	D	E	F
13	A	B	C	D	E	F
14	A	B	C	D	E	F
15	A	B	C	D	E	F

EXERCISE 3: Short Numerical Reasoning

Instructions: Work out and select ONE correct answer for each of the questions.
Mark your answer on the answer sheet.   *Maximum time allowed: 10 minutes*

1

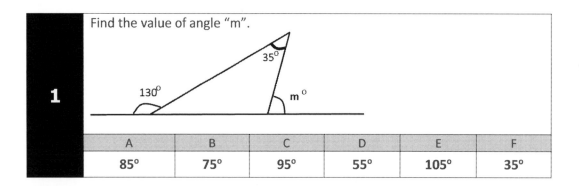

Find the value of angle "m".

35°

130^0

m ^{o}

A	B	C	D	E	F
85°	75°	95°	55°	105°	35°

2

The perimeter of a square is 36 cm. What is the area?

A	B	C	D	E	F
16 cm²	32 cm²	9 cm²	40.5 cm²	81 cm²	12 cm²

3

The cost of 5 pens is £3.50.
What is the cost of 21 pens?

A	B	C	D	E	F
£14.70	£12.50	£12.70	£13.70	£15.70	£21.35

4

9 is a factor of which one of the numbers listed below, between 30 and 40?

A	B	C	D	E	F
18	24	32	34	36	39

5

What is the lowest common multiple of 25, 30 and 40?

A	B	C	D	E	F
5	10	150	300	520	600

6	What is $\sqrt{3\frac{1}{16}}$?					
	A	B	C	D	E	F
	$\frac{7}{4}$	$\frac{49}{16}$	$\frac{7}{2}$	$\frac{1}{4}$	$\frac{2}{4}$	$\frac{1}{2}$

7	What is the highest common factor of 24 and 36?					
	A	B	C	D	E	F
	2	3	4	8	12	16

8	The three sides of a triangle are in the ratio of 2:3:5. The perimeter of the triangle is 100 cm. What is the length of the shortest side?					
	A	B	C	D	E	F
	2 cm	12 cm	20 cm	200 cm	2 mm	20 mm

9	What is the surface area of a cube of length 5 cm?					
	A	B	C	D	E	F
	25 cm²	50 cm²	125 cm²	150 cm²	250 cm²	300 cm²

10	Which of the following is the same as one litre?					
	A	B	C	D	E	F
	10 ml	100 ml	10 cl	100 cm³	1000 cm³	10² cm

11	What is the area of a square with a perimeter of 16 cm?					
	A	B	C	D	E	F
	4 cm	16 cm	14 cm	16 cm²	32 cm²	4 cm²

12 Find the value of the following equation, where x is 2 and y is 3.

$$2x^3 + 5y$$

A	B	C	D	E	F
30	31	23	24	25	13

13 How many thirds are there in 3?

A	B	C	D	E	F
1	3	6	9	12	15

14 What is $\frac{3}{8} of$ 16?

A	B	C	D	E	F
3	4	6	8	16	12

15 Find the missing number "n".

$$\frac{1}{4} + n = \frac{5}{12}$$

A	B	C	D	E	F
$\frac{1}{8}$	$\frac{2}{8}$	$\frac{1}{12}$	$\frac{1}{6}$	$\frac{2}{6}$	$\frac{1}{6}$

Answer Sheet:

1	~~A~~	~~B~~	~~C~~	~~D~~	~~E~~	~~F~~
2	~~A~~	~~B~~	~~C~~	~~D~~	~~E~~	~~F~~
3	~~A~~	~~B~~	~~C~~	~~D~~	~~E~~	~~F~~
4	~~A~~	~~B~~	~~C~~	~~D~~	~~E~~	~~F~~
5	~~A~~	~~B~~	~~C~~	~~D~~	~~E~~	~~F~~
6	~~A~~	~~B~~	~~C~~	~~D~~	~~E~~	~~F~~
7	~~A~~	~~B~~	~~C~~	~~D~~	~~E~~	~~F~~
8	~~A~~	~~B~~	~~C~~	~~D~~	~~E~~	~~F~~
9	~~A~~	~~B~~	~~C~~	~~D~~	~~E~~	~~F~~
10	~~A~~	~~B~~	~~C~~	~~D~~	~~E~~	~~F~~
11	~~A~~	~~B~~	~~C~~	~~D~~	~~E~~	~~F~~
12	~~A~~	~~B~~	~~C~~	~~D~~	~~E~~	~~F~~
13	~~A~~	~~B~~	~~C~~	~~D~~	~~E~~	~~F~~
14	~~A~~	~~B~~	~~C~~	~~D~~	~~E~~	~~F~~
15	~~A~~	~~B~~	~~C~~	~~D~~	~~E~~	~~F~~

EXERCISE 4: Short Numerical Reasoning

Instructions: Work out and select ONE correct answer for each of the questions.
Mark your answer on the answer sheet.   *Maximum time allowed: 10 minutes*

1	Which of these are prime numbers?					
	A	B	C	D	E	F
	1	13	14	15	18	9

2	What is the highest common factor of 35 and 49?					
	A	B	C	D	E	F
	1	3	5	7	9	2

3	What is $\sqrt{7\frac{1}{9}}$?					
	A	B	C	D	E	F
	$\frac{7}{2}$	$\frac{7}{3}$	$\frac{3}{7}$	$\frac{8}{2}$	$2\frac{2}{3}$	$\frac{7}{2}$

4	The three sides of a triangle are in the ratio of 1:3:5. The total length of all three sides is equal to 45 cm. What is the length of the longest side?					
	A	B	C	D	E	F
	15 cm	20 cm	25 cm	30 cm	5 cm	8 cm

5	The number "a" is a multiple of 8 between 60 and 70. The number "b" is a multiple of 9 between 50 and 60. What is **a + b**?					
	A	B	C	D	E	F
	108	118	64	54	70	60

6	How many quarters are there in 4?					
	A	B	C	D	E	F
	1	4	8	12	16	20

7	Work out $\frac{5}{12} - \frac{1}{8}$					
	A	B	C	D	E	F
	$\frac{1}{3}$	$\frac{1}{8}$	$\frac{3}{5}$	$\frac{1}{12}$	$\frac{7}{24}$	$\frac{1}{4}$

8	What is the area of a triangle with a base of 16 cm and height of 6.5cm?					
	A	B	C	D	E	F
	10.4 cm²	14.4 cm²	52 cm²	104 cm²	20.4 cm²	204 cm²

9	What is the product of 2.53 and 10^2?					
	A	B	C	D	E	F
	2.53	25.3	253	2530	201.53	20.153

10	Find the missing number "n". $2\frac{1}{2} \times \frac{1}{n} = \frac{5}{8}$					
	A	B	C	D	E	F
	2	4	6	8	12	1

11	Which one of the below is a triangular number?					
	A	B	C	D	E	F
	1	2	6	7	8	9

12 What is $-3-5$?

A	B	C	D	E	F
-2	-7	-8	2	8	7

13 Find the missing number.

$$0.32 \times \boxed{} = 0.032$$

A	B	C	D	E	F
10	100	1	0.1	0.01	10^3

14 What is 13 x 0.7?

A	B	C	D	E	F
8.1	9.1	81	91	9.4	8.4

15 What is the maximum individual angle in an equilateral triangle?

A	B	C	D	E	F
45°	75°	85°	60°	90°	180°

Answer Sheet:

1	A	B	C	D	E	F
2	A	B	C	D	E	F
3	A	B	C	D	E	F
4	A	B	C	D	E	F
5	A	B	C	D	E	F
6	A	B	C	D	E	F
7	A	B	C	D	E	F
8	A	B	C	D	E	F
9	A	B	C	D	E	F
10	A	B	C	D	E	F
11	A	B	C	D	E	F
12	A	B	C	D	E	F
13	A	B	C	D	E	F
14	A	B	C	D	E	F
15	A	B	C	D	E	F

EXERCISE 5: Short Numerical Reasoning

Instructions: Work out and select ONE correct answer for each of the questions.
Mark your answer on the answer sheet.   *Maximum time allowed: 10 minutes*

1

What is the lowest common multiple of 15 and 8?

A	B	C	D	E	F
30	15	16	90	120	210

2

What of $\frac{2}{5}$ of 500 ml?

A	B	C	D	E	F
200 l	2 ml	2 l	0.2 ml	200 ml	20 ml

3

What is the square root of 625?

A	B	C	D	E	F
15	18	20	25	30	35

4

How many $\frac{1}{8}$ s are in 8?

A	B	C	D	E	F
1	16	64	8	10	100

5

What is $2 \times 3\frac{1}{2}$?

A	B	C	D	E	F
6	7	9	6.5	7.5	$6\frac{1}{2}$

6	Find the value of "x". $15x - 5 = 25$					
	A	B	C	D	E	F
	10	15	5	30	25	2

7	How many rectangular faces does a cuboid have?					
	A	B	C	D	E	F
	4	6	7	8	12	16

8	What is $-30 \div -6$?					
	A	B	C	D	E	F
	5	-5	6	-6	36	-36

9	Find the area of the shaded part of the diagram below.					

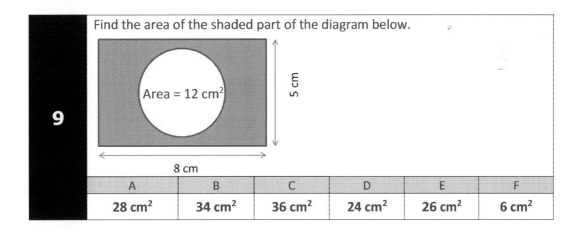

	A	B	C	D	E	F
	28 cm²	34 cm²	36 cm²	24 cm²	26 cm²	6 cm²

10	Find the value of of "p". $30 - 5p = 10$					
	A	B	C	D	E	F
	-4	-6	6	4	-35	-25

11	What is $0.52 \times \frac{2}{20}$?					
	A	B	C	D	E	F
	5.2	0.52	0.052	52	50.2	0.125

12	Five copies of a new book by a famous author are being sold at a local shop every 10 minutes. The book is priced at £5.60. How much money will the shop receive in one hour?					
	A	B	C	D	E	F
	158	30	160	168	178	170

13	The cost of a pen is £0.80 and the cost of a pencil is 30p. How much would it cost to buy 10 pens and 15 pencils?					
	A	B	C	D	E	F
	£12.50	£308	£30.8	£3.80	£125	£1.25

14	John is driving from London and has travelled 111 miles out of the 666 miles he intends. What fraction of the total journey has he completed?					
	A	B	C	D	E	F
	$\frac{1}{6}$	$\frac{1}{3}$	$\frac{2}{3}$	$\frac{1}{4}$	$\frac{3}{4}$	$2\frac{1}{6}$

15	How many 2p coins are required to make £9.80?					
	A	B	C	D	E	F
	49	490	50	512	500	39

Answer Sheet:

1	A	B	C	D	E	F
2	A	B	C	D	E	F
3	A	B	C	D	E	F
4	A	B	C	D	E	F
5	A	B	C	D	E	F
6	A	B	C	D	E	F
7	A	B	C	D	E	F
8	A	B	C	D	E	F
9	A	B	C	D	E	F
10	A	B	C	D	E	F
11	A	B	C	D	E	F
12	A	B	C	D	E	F
13	A	B	C	D	E	F
14	A	B	C	D	E	F
15	A	B	C	D	E	F

EXERCISE 6: Short Numerical Reasoning

Instructions: Work out and select ONE correct answer for each of the questions.
Mark your answer on the answer sheet. *Maximum time allowed: 10 minutes*

1

A car starts at 10:50 AM and completes the journey of 87.5 miles at 1:20 PM. What was the average speed?

A	B	C	D	E	F
35 mph	30 mph	30.5 mph	31.2 mph	40.5 mph	30.25mph

2

The distance between London and Birmingham is 120 miles. If a train has completed 30% of the journey, how many miles of the journey is **remaining**?

A	B	C	D	E	F
82 miles	84 miles	72 miles	48 miles	24 miles	62 miles

3

Find the angle marked m°

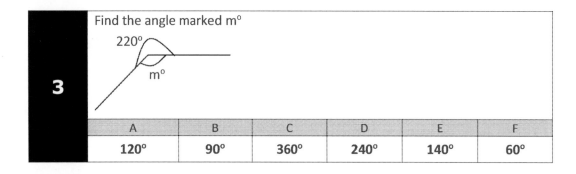

A	B	C	D	E	F
120°	90°	360°	240°	140°	60°

4

A bag of apples weigh 3 kg. If the average weight of an apple is 250 grams, how many apples are there in the bag?

A	B	C	D	E	F
8	10	12	14	15	16

Mastering 11+ / MATHS / Practice Book TWO

5 What is $3 \times (12 - 4) \div 3$?

A	B	C	D	E	F
32	10.6	11	8	6	14

6 How many days is 168 hours?

A	B	C	D	E	F
3	7	8	9	4.5	6.5

7 Find the value of "x".

$100 - 3x = 10$

A	B	C	D	E	F
-30	-3	-13	-90	90	30

8 What is $10 \times 1\frac{3}{4}$?

A	B	C	D	E	F
101.75	17.5	175	10.75	11.75	$10\frac{3}{4}$

9 What is the square root of 289?

A	B	C	D	E	F
13	16	17	23	12	15

10 How many $\frac{1}{16}$ s are in 8?

A	B	C	D	E	F
16	32	64	128	256	512

11	Raj is saving all his pocket money to buy the full football kit of his favourite club, which costs £84. His pocket money is £12 every **two** weeks. How many weeks would it take Raj to save enough to buy the kit?					
	A	B	C	D	E	F
	7	9	11	13	14	16

12	What is the missing number? $$\frac{2 + 3^3 - 5^2}{?} = 1$$					
	A	B	C	D	E	F
	-14	3	4	5	6	7

13	Which of the following percentages of "x" does the value of "y" represent in the following equation? $0.25\, x = y$					
	A	B	C	D	E	F
	4%	40%	50%	25%	2.5%	20%

14	Reduce 6 litre by 25%					
	A	B	C	D	E	F
	1.5 l	7.5 l	6 l	4.5 l	2.5 l	2.85 l

15	You are asked to think of a number, double it and then multiply by 7. Divide the whole thing by 12. Which of the following equations represent this?					
	A	B	C	D	E	F
	$\dfrac{14n}{12}$	$\dfrac{2n + 7}{12}$	$\dfrac{7n^2}{12}$	$\dfrac{7n}{12}$	$\dfrac{n + n \times 7}{12}$	$\dfrac{n + n}{12}$

Answer Sheet:

	A	B	C	D	E	F
1	A	B	C	D	E	F
2	A	B	C	D	E	F
3	A	B	C	D	E	F
4	A	B	C	D	E	F
5	A	B	C	D	E	F
6	A	B	C	D	E	F
7	A	B	C	D	E	F
8	A	B	C	D	E	F
9	A	B	C	D	E	F
10	A	B	C	D	E	F
11	A	B	C	D	E	F
12	A	B	C	D	E	F
13	A	B	C	D	E	F
14	A	B	C	D	E	F
15	A	B	C	D	E	F

EXERCISE 7: Short Numerical Reasoning

Instructions: Work out and select ONE correct answer for each of the questions.
Mark your answer on the answer sheet.   *Maximum time allowed: 10 minutes*

1	What is 5% of £360?					
	A	B	C	D	E	F
	£180	£251	£190	£18	£19	£19.50

2	Find the value of angle "p".					
	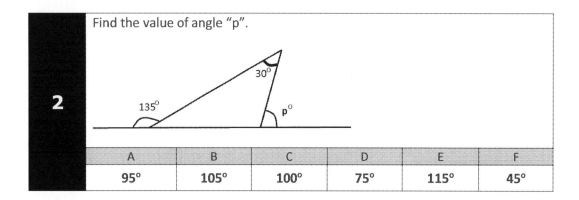					
	A	B	C	D	E	F
	95°	105°	100°	75°	115°	45°

3	Using the two equations below, find the value of "b". 6a + 5 = 35 5b=a					
	A	B	C	D	E	F
	25	6	5	30	35	1

4	What is the missing number? $\dfrac{(2^3 + 10)}{?} = 2$					
	A	B	C	D	E	F
	8	6	3	9	12	18

5	What is $7 \times 0.01 + 5 \times 0.1$?					
	A	B	C	D	E	F
	0.57	0.75	0.12	0.751	0.571	7.5

6	Which 3-dimensional shape has a square base and 4 triangular faces?					
	A	B	C	D	E	F
	Rectangular Pyramid	Sphere	Rectangular Prism	Cuboid	Cube	Cone

7	The area of the rectangle below is 100 cm². Find the value of "x".

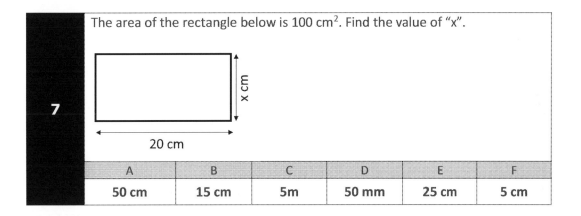

20 cm

x cm

	A	B	C	D	E	F
	50 cm	15 cm	5m	50 mm	25 cm	5 cm

8	A factory used 150 oranges to make 50 bottles of 250 ml orange juice. How many oranges is that per bottle?					
	A	B	C	D	E	F
	7.5	5	4	3	2	Can't say

9	Which of the following signs make the following equation true?

$150 \boxed{} 10.5 \times 10$

	A	B	C	D	E	F
	+	X	=	<	>	÷

10	What is 787 ÷ 7, rounded to the nearest 10th?					
	A	B	C	D	E	F
	110	112	115	120	112.43	112.42

11 What is the missing time in the sequence below?

10:10 AM	10:50 AM	11:30 AM	12:10 PM	?

A	B	C	D	E	F
12:50 AM	12:45 AM	13:00	12:15 PM	12:50 PM	12:55 PM

12 The monthly income of a family is £4200. They spend $\frac{2}{3}$ of it, saving the rest. How much is the monthly saving?

A	B	C	D	E	F
£2800	£280	£2850	£1400	£1620	£1680

13 How many 10p coins are required to make £10?

A	B	C	D	E	F
100	1000	150	1500	10	50

14 What is the angle between the two hands of a clock showing 6'o clock?

A	B	C	D	E	F
60°	80°	90°	120°	160°	180°

15 What is the product of 0.765 and 10^2?

A	B	C	D	E	F
0.0765	0.00765	7.65	76.5	765	7650

Answer Sheet:

1	~~A~~	~~B~~	~~C~~	~~D~~	~~E~~	~~F~~
2	~~A~~	~~B~~	~~C~~	~~D~~	~~E~~	~~F~~
3	~~A~~	~~B~~	~~C~~	~~D~~	~~E~~	~~F~~
4	~~A~~	~~B~~	~~C~~	~~D~~	~~E~~	~~F~~
5	~~A~~	~~B~~	~~C~~	~~D~~	~~E~~	~~F~~
6	~~A~~	~~B~~	~~C~~	~~D~~	~~E~~	~~F~~
7	~~A~~	~~B~~	~~C~~	~~D~~	~~E~~	~~F~~
8	~~A~~	~~B~~	~~C~~	~~D~~	~~E~~	~~F~~
9	~~A~~	~~B~~	~~C~~	~~D~~	~~E~~	~~F~~
10	~~A~~	~~B~~	~~C~~	~~D~~	~~E~~	~~F~~
11	~~A~~	~~B~~	~~C~~	~~D~~	~~E~~	~~F~~
12	~~A~~	~~B~~	~~C~~	~~D~~	~~E~~	~~F~~
13	~~A~~	~~B~~	~~C~~	~~D~~	~~E~~	~~F~~
14	~~A~~	~~B~~	~~C~~	~~D~~	~~E~~	~~F~~
15	~~A~~	~~B~~	~~C~~	~~D~~	~~E~~	~~F~~

EXERCISE 8: Short Numerical Reasoning

Instructions: Work out and select ONE correct answer for each of the questions.

Mark your answer on the answer sheet.   *Maximum time allowed: 10 minutes*

1

Sarah is 5 years older than her sister Michelle.
If "x" is Michelle's age and "y" is Sarah's, which of the following equation represent the above statement accurately?

A	B	C	D	E	F
$y = 5x$	$y = \dfrac{x}{5}$	$x = y + 5$	$y = x + 5$	$x = \dfrac{y}{5}$	$x + y = 5$

2

What is the missing number?

$$\frac{(2^3 + 5^2)}{?} = 11$$

A	B	C	D	E	F
2	3	4	6	9	1

3

What is $2\frac{1}{2}$ of £100?

A	B	C	D	E	F
25	2.5	250	0.25	26	52

4

What is the missing time in the sequence below?

10:10 AM   9:30 AM   8:50 AM   ?   7:30 AM

A	B	C	D	E	F
8:05 AM	8:10 PM	08:00 AM	07:10 AM	07:50 AM	08:10 AM

5

What is $9 \times 0.01 + 2 \times 0.1$?

A	B	C	D	E	F
0.92	0.29	0.092	2.09	2.90	9.02

6	Which of the following signs make the following equation true? $12 \quad \boxed{} \quad 1.5 \times 20$					
	A	B	C	D	E	F
	+	X	=	<	>	÷

7	The perimeter of a rectangle is 30 cm and the longest side measures 10 cm. What is the area of the rectangle?					
	A	B	C	D	E	F
	300 cm²	100 cm²	500 cm²	50 cm²	30 cm²	30 cm²

8	What is $\sqrt{5\frac{4}{9}}$?					
	A	B	C	D	E	F
	$\sqrt{5\frac{2}{3}}$	$\sqrt{5\frac{4}{9}}$	$\sqrt{5\frac{4}{9}}$	$\sqrt{\frac{7}{3}}$	$2\frac{1}{3}$	$\frac{3}{7}$

9	Three brothers share the prize money of £270,000 in the ratio of 2:3:4. What was the smallest share of the three?					
	A	B	C	D	E	F
	£30,000	£60,000	£90,000	£120,000	£150,000	£180,000

10	The McDonald family earns a total of £5,000 a month. They save 15% of it every month. What is the **annual** saving?					
	A	B	C	D	E	F
	£9000	£900	£90	£750	£75	£7500

11	What is the product of 0.2 and 0.3?					
	A	B	C	D	E	F
	0.5	0.6	0.05	0.06	0.006	0.23

12	"m" is a factor of 9 between 80 and 85 "n" is a factor of 10 between 95 and 105 What is $n - m$?

A	B	C	D	E	F
71	81	91	19	90	-10

13	What is the value of "n" in the following equation? $9^n = 81$

A	B	C	D	E	F
9	8	6	3	2	0

14	A party organiser uses the following formula to calculate the cost to host a birthday party. **Cost = £7.00 x number of children + £50** If Mr. Robinson was told it would cost him £99 to host his son's party, how many children were to attend the party?

A	B	C	D	E	F
7	8	9	10	11	12

15	What is $-2 \times \frac{1}{2}$?

A	B	C	D	E	F
-2.5	-2	-1	1	0.5	$-2\frac{1}{2}$

Answer Sheet:

1	A	B	C	D	E	F
2	A	B	C	D	E	F
3	A	B	C	D	E	F
4	A	B	C	D	E	F
5	A	B	C	D	E	F
6	A	B	C	D	E	F
7	A	B	C	D	E	F
8	A	B	C	D	E	F
9	A	B	C	D	E	F
10	A	B	C	D	E	F
11	A	B	C	D	E	F
12	A	B	C	D	E	F
13	A	B	C	D	E	F
14	A	B	C	D	E	F
15	A	B	C	D	E	F

EXERCISE 9: Short Numerical Reasoning

Instructions: **Work out and select ONE correct answer for each of the questions.**
Mark your answer on the answer sheet. *Maximum time allowed: 10 minutes*

1

What is the value of missing number "n"?

$$\frac{(2^2 + n)}{10} = 10.3$$

A	B	C	D	E	F
10	20	50	90	100	99

2

What is 18% of £2500?

A	B	C	D	E	F
£450	£465	£425	£525	£550	£565

3

Dan weights twice as much as Ian. Their total weight is 90 kg.
What is Ian's weight?

A	B	C	D	E	F
35 kg	25 kg	30 kg	60 kg	70 kg	10 kg

4

What is the next number in the sequence?

-3   -8   -4   -9   -5   -10   ?

A	B	C	D	E	F
-6	-5	-8	-9	-15	-11

5

The angle between two hands of a clock is 180°.
What is the time on the clock?

A	B	C	D	E	F
3:00 AM	6:00 PM	5:00 AM	4:00 PM	8:00 AM	09:00 AM

6	What is $\dfrac{\sqrt{81}}{3}$?					
	A	B	C	D	E	F
	9	6	3	1	¼	¾

7	What is $0 \times 1\frac{1}{2}$?					
	A	B	C	D	E	F
	1.5	$1\frac{1}{2}$	0	1.25	1	1.55

8	What is the lowest common multiple of 3 and 8?					
	A	B	C	D	E	F
	3	8	9	18	21	24

9	What is $\dfrac{\sqrt{169}}{3}$?					
	A	B	C	D	E	F
	$4\frac{1}{3}$	4	3	9	½	7

10	What is $0.3 - 0.29$?					
	A	B	C	D	E	F
	0.1	0.19	-0.11	-0.1	0.01	0.11

11	The sum of two consecutive numbers is 15. One of the two numbers is a prime number between 5 and 8. What is the product of the two numbers?					
	A	B	C	D	E	F
	56	49	13	15	40	75

12 What is the next number in the sequence?

2   3   5   7   11   13   ?

A	B	C	D	E	F
14	15	16	17	19	21

13 What is the value of "n" in the following equation?

$$10^n = 110 - (2 \times 5)$$

A	B	C	D	E	F
0	1	2	3	4	5

14 What is $2\frac{1}{3}$ of 9kg?

A	B	C	D	E	F
7 kg	3.33 kg	18 kg	18.66 kg	5.33 kg	21 kg

15 In what year would a man born in 1977 be 33 years old?

A	B	C	D	E	F
2000	1999	2001	2010	2011	2009

Answer Sheet:

1	A	B	C	D	E	F
2	A	B	C	D	E	F
3	A	B	C	D	E	F
4	A	B	C	D	E	F
5	A	B	C	D	E	F
6	A	B	C	D	E	F
7	A	B	C	D	E	F
8	A	B	C	D	E	F
9	A	B	C	D	E	F
10	A	B	C	D	E	F
11	A	B	C	D	E	F
12	A	B	C	D	E	F
13	A	B	C	D	E	F
14	A	B	C	D	E	F
15	A	B	C	D	E	F

EXERCISE 10: Short Numerical Reasoning

Instructions: Work out and select ONE correct answer for each of the questions.
Mark your answer on the answer sheet.   *Maximum time allowed: 10 minutes*

1 Which of the following equation will give the largest value, if the value of "x" is 5?

A	B	C	D	E	F
$n^2 - 3n$	$\dfrac{n}{n+1}$	$\dfrac{n+1}{n}$	$\dfrac{3n}{n-4}$	$\dfrac{n^2}{3n}$	$n - 2n$

2 There are 5 red balls and 2 blue balls in a bag. What are the odds of someone pulling out a blue ball from the bag, represented as a fraction?

A	B	C	D	E	F
$\dfrac{1}{2}$	$\dfrac{5}{2}$	$\dfrac{2}{5}$	$\dfrac{7}{2}$	$\dfrac{1}{7}$	$\dfrac{2}{7}$

3 Find the value of "m" in the equation below.

$5 + 6m^2 = 11$

A	B	C	D	E	F
5	25	0	1	6	3

4 The word **EAST** is represented by numbers 5190. Which of the following represent the word **TEASE?**

A	B	C	D	E	F
5190	51905	05195	9051	1590	15091

5 Sum of the two consecutive numbers is 23. One of the two numbers is a prime number between 9 and 15. Find the product of the two numbers?

A	B	C	D	E	F
121	131	141	151	123	132

6	What is $\dfrac{\sqrt{144}}{12}$?					
	A	B	C	D	E	F
	0	1	12	11	12.12	13

7	What is $3 \times 3\frac{1}{3}$?					
	A	B	C	D	E	F
	1	9	3	10	9.5	9.33

8	Rob has saved £12,300 in a bank account. The bank pays 3% interest per annum. How much interest would that be for a year?					
	A	B	C	D	E	F
	£396	£369	£386	£368	£3699	£3690

9	The price of petrol over the last decade has increased from 60p to 120p. What is this represented as a percentage?					
	A	B	C	D	E	F
	20%	50%	100%	200%	250%	25%

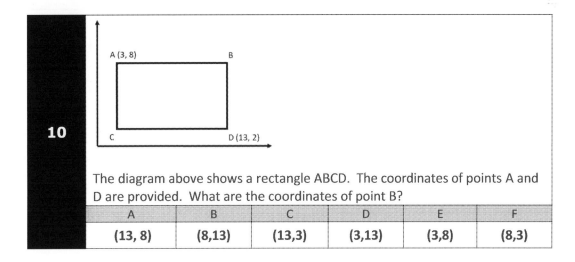

10	The diagram above shows a rectangle ABCD. The coordinates of points A and D are provided. What are the coordinates of point B?					
	A	B	C	D	E	F
	(13, 8)	(8,13)	(13,3)	(3,13)	(3,8)	(8,3)

11 Find the value of the following expression when the value of "x" is 8.

$(7x - 49)$

A	B	C	D	E	F
-49	14	-14	7	0	-98

12 Michael celebrated his 14th birthday on 15th December 2014.
How old will be on 15th December 2021?

A	B	C	D	E	F
20	21	22	18	15	14

13 What is the missing number?

$5 \times \boxed{} + 20 = 95$

A	B	C	D	E	F
75	70	4	5	10	15

14 The temperature inside a car being driven on a motorway is 16°C. The outside temperature is 20°C colder. What is the outside temperature?

A	B	C	D	E	F
36°C	4°C	-14°C	-36°C	-4°C	-6°C

15 A charity event at a local school raised £782.28. How much is this rounded to the nearest tenth?

A	B	C	D	E	F
£782.3	£782.2	£782	£783	£780	£790

Answer Sheet:

1	A	B	C	D	E	F
2	A	B	C	D	E	F
3	A	B	C	D	E	F
4	A	B	C	D	E	F
5	A	B	C	D	E	F
6	A	B	C	D	E	F
7	A	B	C	D	E	F
8	A	B	C	D	E	F
9	A	B	C	D	E	F
10	A	B	C	D	E	F
11	A	B	C	D	E	F
12	A	B	C	D	E	F
13	A	B	C	D	E	F
14	A	B	C	D	E	F
15	A	B	C	D	E	F

This page is intentionally left blank

LONG MATHS

EXERCISE 11: Multipart Numerical Reasoning

Instructions: Work out and mark your answers by filling the appropriate grids on the answer sheet. Use a separate sheet for your workings.

Maximum time allowed: 5 minutes

Sam earns an annual salary of £75,000 as an IT project manager.

The tax on this income is charged as per the rules below:
- *No tax on the first £10,000*
- *20% tax on income between £10,001 and £40,000*
- *40% tax on income above £40,000*

| 1 | How much tax will Sam pay in a year? Round it to the nearest ten. |

| 2 | How much is Sam's net salary? Round it to the nearest ten.
Net salary = annual salary – tax deducted |

| 3 | What is Sam's monthly net salary, rounded to the nearest ten? |

| 4 | If Sam also received an additional bonus payment of £15,000, how much more tax, rounded to the nearest pound, he will have to pay? |

| 5 | Express bonus payment as a percentage of the salary? Round the answer to the nearest unit. |

Answer Sheet – Exercise 11

Question Number	Answer Grid	Question Number	Answer Grid
1	0 0 0 0 0 1 1 1 1 1 2 2 2 2 2 3 3 3 3 3 4 4 4 4 4 5 5 5 5 5 6 6 6 6 6 7 7 7 7 7 8 8 8 8 8 9 9 9 9 9	4	0 0 0 0 0 1 1 1 1 1 2 2 2 2 2 3 3 3 3 3 4 4 4 4 4 5 5 5 5 5 6 6 6 6 6 7 7 7 7 7 8 8 8 8 8 9 9 9 9 9
2	0 0 0 0 0 1 1 1 1 1 2 2 2 2 2 3 3 3 3 3 4 4 4 4 4 5 5 5 5 5 6 6 6 6 6 7 7 7 7 7 8 8 8 8 8 9 9 9 9 9	5	0 0 0 0 0 1 1 1 1 1 2 2 2 2 2 3 3 3 3 3 4 4 4 4 4 5 5 5 5 5 6 6 6 6 6 7 7 7 7 7 8 8 8 8 8 9 9 9 9 9
3	0 0 0 0 0 1 1 1 1 1 2 2 2 2 2 3 3 3 3 3 4 4 4 4 4 5 5 5 5 5 6 6 6 6 6 7 7 7 7 7 8 8 8 8 8 9 9 9 9 9		

Instructions: Work out and mark your answers by filling the appropriate grids on the answer sheet. Use a separate sheet for your workings.

Maximum time allowed: 5 minutes

Here is the menu from a local café.

The Essex Café

Starters:

Tomato Soup……………………………	£2.25
Goulash Soup…………………………....	£3.00

Main Course:

Fish & Chips with peas …………………...	£4.50
Jacket Potato with cheese filling ………...	£3.99
Grilled Salmon with baby potatoes ……...	£4.99
Penne Pasta ……………………………....	£3.99

Desserts:

Ice Cream – Vanilla/Strawberry ………...	£1.50
Hot Apple Pie...	£1.20
Rice Pudding …………………………….	£1.25

Drinks:

Tea ……………………………………..	£0.80
Coffee …………………………………….	£0.90
Orange Juice ………………………………	£1.20
Coke ……………………………………....	£0.60

Use the menu above to answer questions on the next page.

1	How much would it cost John to have the following? Goulash Soup, Penne Pasta and a Coke

2	If John had £10, how much money would he have left after paying for the meal?

3	Carlo has £7.50. He wants to buy Grilled Salmon and orange juice with a dessert. What is the price of the most expensive dessert he can buy?

4	Guillaume buys 10 pots of rice pudding and 5 apple pies. How much would it cost him?

5	How much will the most expensive meal cost if you have to pick a starter, a main course, a dessert and a drink?

Answer Sheet – Exercise 12

Question Number	Answer Grid	Question Number	Answer Grid
1	Grid 1 (below)	4	Grid 4 (below)
2	Grid 2 (below)	5	Grid 5 (below)
3	Grid 3 (below)		

1

0	0	0	0	0	.	0	0
1	1	1	1	1	.	1	1
2	2	2	2	2	.	2	2
3	3	3	3	3	.	3	3
4	4	4	4	4	.	4	4
5	5	5	5	5	.	5	5
6	6	6	6	6	.	6	6
7	7	7	7	7	.	7	7
8	8	8	8	8	.	8	8
9	9	9	9	9	.	9	9

4

0	0	0	0	0	.	0	0
1	1	1	1	1	.	1	1
2	2	2	2	2	.	2	2
3	3	3	3	3	.	3	3
4	4	4	4	4	.	4	4
5	5	5	5	5	.	5	5
6	6	6	6	6	.	6	6
7	7	7	7	7	.	7	7
8	8	8	8	8	.	8	8
9	9	9	9	9	.	9	9

2

0	0	0	0	0	.	0	0
1	1	1	1	1	.	1	1
2	2	2	2	2	.	2	2
3	3	3	3	3	.	3	3
4	4	4	4	4	.	4	4
5	5	5	5	5	.	5	5
6	6	6	6	6	.	6	6
7	7	7	7	7	.	7	7
8	8	8	8	8	.	8	8
9	9	9	9	9	.	9	9

5

0	0	0	0	0	.	0	0
1	1	1	1	1	.	1	1
2	2	2	2	2	.	2	2
3	3	3	3	3	.	3	3
4	4	4	4	4	.	4	4
5	5	5	5	5	.	5	5
6	6	6	6	6	.	6	6
7	7	7	7	7	.	7	7
8	8	8	8	8	.	8	8
9	9	9	9	9	.	9	9

3

0	0	0	0	0	.	0	0
1	1	1	1	1	.	1	1
2	2	2	2	2	.	2	2
3	3	3	3	3	.	3	3
4	4	4	4	4	.	4	4
5	5	5	5	5	.	5	5
6	6	6	6	6	.	6	6
7	7	7	7	7	.	7	7
8	8	8	8	8	.	8	8
9	9	9	9	9	.	9	9

EXERCISE 13: Multipart Numerical Reasoning

Instructions: Work out and mark your answers by filling the appropriate grids on the answer sheet. Use a separate sheet for your workings.

Maximum time allowed: 5 minutes

The diagram shows a kite and is not drawn to scale. The lengths are in centimetres.

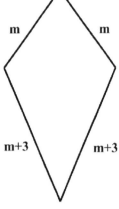

1	What is the perimeter of the kite above, if the value of **m** is 7 cm?

2	What is the perimeter of the kite if the value of **m** is 14 cm?

3	What is the value of **m**, if the perimeter of the kite is 126 cm?

4	What is the value of **m**, if the perimeter of the kite is 46 cm?

5	What is the value of **m**, if the perimeter of the kite is 26 cm?

Answer Sheet – Exercise 13

Question Number	Answer Grid	Question Number	Answer Grid
1		**4**	
2		**5**	
3			

EXERCISE 14: Multipart Numerical Reasoning

Instructions: Work out and mark your answers by filling the appropriate grids on the answer sheet. Use a separate sheet for your workings.

Maximum time allowed: 5 minutes

The graph shows the temperatures measured on two days, every hour, between 6:00 AM and 6:00 PM.

The top line on the graph shows the temperature measured on 14th September while the bottom line show the temperature measured on 22nd December.

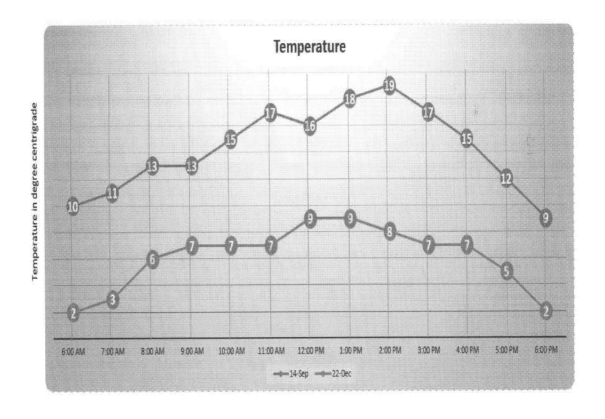

1   What was the temperature at 11:00 AM on 14th September?

2   What was the highest temperature recorded on 22nd December?

3   By how many degrees did the temperature drop by, between 12 noon and 5:00 PM on 22nd December?

4   What was the difference in temperatures across the two days, as at 2:00 PM?

5   How many degrees did the temperature go up by, between 12 noon and 2:00 PM on 14th September?

Answer Sheet – Exercise 14

Question Number	Answer Grid	Question Number	Answer Grid
1	(answer grid: rows 0–9, 5 columns of bubbles)	**4**	(answer grid: rows 0–9, 5 columns of bubbles)
2	(answer grid: rows 0–9, 5 columns of bubbles)	**5**	(answer grid: rows 0–9, 5 columns of bubbles)
3	(answer grid: rows 0–9, 5 columns of bubbles)		

EXERCISE 15: Multipart Numerical Reasoning

Instructions: Work out and mark your answers by filling the appropriate grids on the answer sheet. Use a separate sheet for your workings.

Maximum time allowed: 5 minutes

One of the top football clubs in the country has a stadium with a capacity to host 40,000 spectators. The club plays 25 games at the stadium in a year.

The average ticket price for a game is £40.

The club also offers an annual ticket that costs £800 and will allow the holder to see all the 25 games. The annual ticket also provides discounts on club's merchandise and on the tickets for away games.

1	How much it would cost for someone to see all the games in a year?

2	How much expensive is this in comparison to buying an annual ticket?

3	The club has sold 250 annual tickets this season. How much money is this worth to the club?

4	What additional revenue would the club raise by increasing the price of the annual tickets by 10%?

5	The club would like to increase the capacity of the stadium by 20% in 5 years' time. What is the additional revenue the club would generate as a result of this increased capacity, per game? Assume the ticket prices remain unchanged.

Answer Sheet – Exercise 15

Question Number	Answer Grid	Question Number	Answer Grid
1	(answer grid bubbles 0–9)	4	(answer grid bubbles 0–9)
2	(answer grid bubbles 0–9)	5	(answer grid bubbles 0–9)
3	(answer grid bubbles 0–9)		

EXERCISE 16: Multipart Numerical Reasoning

Instructions: Work out and mark your answers by filling the appropriate grids on the answer sheet. Use a separate sheet for your workings.

Maximum time allowed: 5 minutes

The diagram below is not drawn accurately but PQR is a right angled triangle. The square fits exactly inside the triangle.

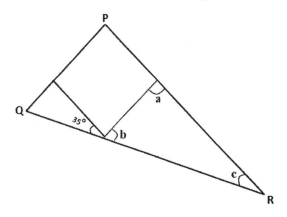

1	Find the value of angle "a".

2	Find the value of angle "b".

3	Find the value of angle "c".

4	Evaluate $3a + 2b - c$

5	Evaluate $a + b + c$

Answer Sheet – Exercise 16

Question Number	Answer Grid	Question Number	Answer Grid
1		4	
2		5	
3			

EXERCISE 17: Multipart Numerical Reasoning

Instructions: Work out and mark your answers by filling the appropriate grids on the answer sheet. Use a separate sheet for your workings.

Maximum time allowed: 5 minutes

The table below shows the summary results of 25 students in a class.

Every cell shows the number of students getting the corresponding levels in Maths and English.

No. of students graded Level 3 in both English & Maths

		Mathematics			
		Level 3	Level 4	Level 5	Level 6
English	Level 3	1	5	1	1
	Level 4	6	0	1	0
	Level 5	2	3	2	1
	Level 6	1	0	0	1

1 How many children were graded Level 6 in Mathematics?

2 How many children were graded Level 6 either in Mathematics or English?

3 How many children had the same level in both Maths and English?

4 How many children had higher grade in English than Maths?

5 How many children had higher grade in Maths than English?

Answer Sheet – Exercise 17

Question Number	Answer Grid	Question Number	Answer Grid
1	0 0 0 0 0 1 1 1 1 1 2 2 2 2 2 3 3 3 3 3 4 4 4 4 4 5 5 5 5 5 6 6 6 6 6 7 7 7 7 7 8 8 8 8 8 9 9 9 9 9	4	0 0 0 0 0 1 1 1 1 1 2 2 2 2 2 3 3 3 3 3 4 4 4 4 4 5 5 5 5 5 6 6 6 6 6 7 7 7 7 7 8 8 8 8 8 9 9 9 9 9
2	0 0 0 0 0 1 1 1 1 1 2 2 2 2 2 3 3 3 3 3 4 4 4 4 4 5 5 5 5 5 6 6 6 6 6 7 7 7 7 7 8 8 8 8 8 9 9 9 9 9	5	0 0 0 0 0 1 1 1 1 1 2 2 2 2 2 3 3 3 3 3 4 4 4 4 4 5 5 5 5 5 6 6 6 6 6 7 7 7 7 7 8 8 8 8 8 9 9 9 9 9
3	0 0 0 0 0 1 1 1 1 1 2 2 2 2 2 3 3 3 3 3 4 4 4 4 4 5 5 5 5 5 6 6 6 6 6 7 7 7 7 7 8 8 8 8 8 9 9 9 9 9		

EXERCISE 18: Multipart Numerical Reasoning

Instructions: Work out and mark your answers by filling the appropriate grids on the answer sheet. Use a separate sheet for your workings.

Maximum time allowed: 5 minutes

The table below shows the temperatures in 8 cities recorded on 10th of November, last year.

City	Temperature in ^{o}C
London	$9^{o}C$
Paris	$7^{o}C$
New York	$7^{o}C$
Vienna	$4^{o}C$
Munich	$7^{o}C$
Dubai	$24^{o}C$
Zurich	$3^{o}C$
New Delhi	$19^{o}C$

1	Find the mode.
2	What is the median?
3	Calculate the mean value.
4	Calculate the range?
5	What is the product of mode and median?

Answer Sheet – Exercise 18

Question Number	Answer Grid	Question Number	Answer Grid
1	(answer grid: digits 0–9, five columns, decimal point, two columns)	**4**	(answer grid: digits 0–9, five columns, decimal point, two columns)
2	(answer grid: digits 0–9, five columns, decimal point, two columns)	**5**	(answer grid: digits 0–9, five columns, decimal point, two columns)
3	(answer grid: digits 0–9, five columns, decimal point, two columns)		

EXERCISE 19: Multipart Numerical Reasoning

Instructions: **Work out and mark your answers by filling the appropriate grids on the answer sheet. Use a separate sheet for your workings.**

Maximum time allowed: 5 minutes

A popular shop is selling a games console for £320. It costs the shop £200 for every console.

1	What is the profit as a percentage of the cost?

2	How much profit would be generated by selling 125 units?

3	The shop charges Value Added Tax (VAT) for every unit sold at 20%. What is the total price a customer would pay including the VAT?

4	The ratio between number of consoles sold during week days and weekend is 3:4. If the total number of consoles sold in a week is 210, how many were sold over the weekend?

5	What is the total profit generated by sales over a weekend?

Answer Sheet – Exercise 19

Question Number	Answer Grid	Question Number	Answer Grid
1		**4**	
2		**5**	
3			

EXERCISE 20: Multipart Numerical Reasoning

Instructions: Work out and mark your answers by filling the appropriate grids on the answer sheet. Use a separate sheet for your workings.

Maximum time allowed: 5 minutes

Here is a number pyramid. Every number is the sum of two numbers directly below them.

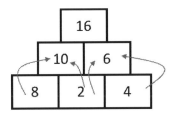

Answer the following questions.

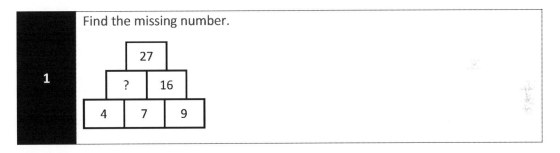

Find the missing number.

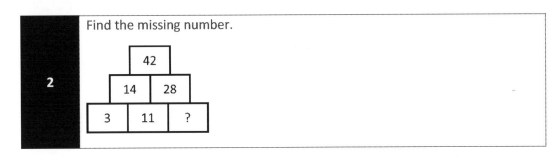

Find the missing number.

3 Find the missing number.

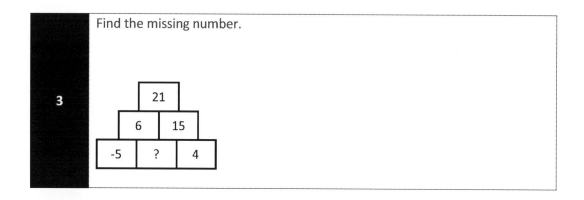

4 Find the missing number.

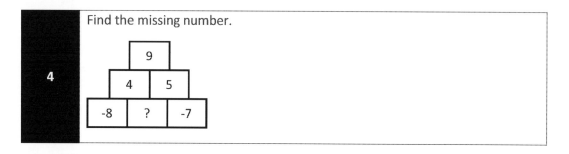

5 Find the missing number.

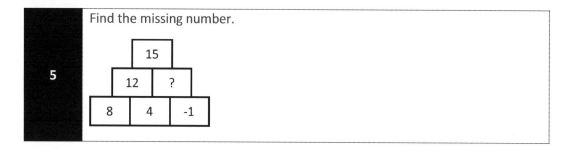

Answer Sheet – Exercise 20

Question Number	Answer Grid	Question Number	Answer Grid
1		**4**	
2		**5**	
3			

This page is intentionally left blank.

ANSWER MATCHING

EXERCISE 21: Answer Matching

Instructions: Work out and match the answers to the appropriate options. Use a separate sheet for your workings.

Maximum time allowed: 5 minutes

ANSWERS

A	7	B	730	C	720	D	80	E	-13
F	72	G	6	H	14	I	-11	J	11

QUESTIONS

1	What is the first perfect number?
2	The Perimeter of a regular shape is 49 cm and each side is 7cm in length. How many sides has the shape got?
3	What is the missing number? $99 \div \boxed{} = 13 - 4$
4	What is the next term in the following sequence? 13, 7, 1, -5, ….
5	Which number between 60 and 80 is a multiple of both 3 and 8?
6	How long is the journey in minutes that began at 5:30 AM and concluded at 5:40 PM?
7	Rubiya was born on 12th February 2003. How old will she be on 12th February 2017?
8	What is 75% of £960?
9	What is $-6 - 7$?
10	Seven boys took a Maths test and the results were 78, 71, 91, 82, 76, and 82. What is the average score?

Answer Sheet

Question Number	A	B	C	D	E	F	G	H	I	J
1	☐	☐	☐	☐	☐	☐	☐	☐	☐	☐
2	☐	☐	☐	☐	☐	☐	☐	☐	☐	☐
3	☐	☐	☐	☐	☐	☐	☐	☐	☐	☐
4	☐	☐	☐	☐	☐	☐	☐	☐	☐	☐
5	☐	☐	☐	☐	☐	☐	☐	☐	☐	☐
6	☐	☐	☐	☐	☐	☐	☐	☐	☐	☐
7	☐	☐	☐	☐	☐	☐	☐	☐	☐	☐
8	☐	☐	☐	☐	☐	☐	☐	☐	☐	☐
9	☐	☐	☐	☐	☐	☐	☐	☐	☐	☐
10	☐	☐	☐	☐	☐	☐	☐	☐	☐	☐

EXERCISE 22: Answer Matching

Instructions: Work out and match the answers to the appropriate options. Use a separate sheet for your workings.

Maximum time allowed: 5 minutes

ANSWERS:

A	90	B	200	C	20	D	50	E	4
F	5	G	180	H	60	I	84	J	6

QUESTIONS

1	What is the value of straight angle?
2	How many days are in 12 weeks?
3	A 500 ml drink is made by mixing two parts of squash to three parts of water. How much of the drink is squash?
4	A quadrilateral shape has angles of 115°, 65° and 90°. What is the value of the 4th angle?
5	What is the missing number? $75 \div \boxed{} = 23 - 8$
6	Jemma has got 15 questions out of 25 correct in her English test. What is her score as a percentage?
7	What is the square root of 400?
8	How many factors does the number 32 have?
9	What is the perimeter of a pentagon whose sides are 10 cm?
10	Find the value of "x" in the following equation. $5x + 3 = 23$

Answer Sheet

Question Number	A	B	C	D	E	F	G	H	I	J
1	A	B	C	D	E	F	G	H	I	J
2	A	B	C	D	E	F	G	H	I	J
3	A	B	C	D	E	F	G	H	I	J
4	A	B	C	D	E	F	G	H	I	J
5	A	B	C	D	E	F	G	H	I	J
6	A	B	C	D	E	F	G	H	I	J
7	A	B	C	D	E	F	G	H	I	J
8	A	B	C	D	E	F	G	H	I	J
9	A	B	C	D	E	F	G	H	I	J
10	A	B	C	D	E	F	G	H	I	J

EXERCISE 23: Answer Matching

Instructions: Work out and match the answers to the appropriate options. Use a separate sheet for your workings.

Maximum time allowed: 5 minutes

ANSWERS:

A	35	B	7	C	414	D	121	E	24
F	20	G	30	H	192	I	180	J	64

QUESTIONS:

1	How many hours are in 8 days?
2	What is 23% of 1800?
3	A right angled triangle has angles of 90° and 55°. What is the value of the third angle?
4	Harry scored 80% in a maths test of 25 questions. How many questions out of 25 did he get right?
5	What is the 10th multiple of 18?
6	What is eleven squared?
7	Convert 0.3 cm^2 into mm^2
8	What is the area of a square whose perimeter is 32 cm?
9	Find the first multiple of 8 which is also a multiple of 6.
10	Find the value of "x" in the following equation. $7x - 3 = 46$

Answer Sheet

Question Number	A	B	C	D	E	F	G	H	I	J
1	⊏⊐	⊏⊐	⊏⊐	⊏⊐	⊏⊐	⊏⊐	⊏⊐	⊏⊐	⊏⊐	⊏⊐
2	⊏⊐	⊏⊐	⊏⊐	⊏⊐	⊏⊐	⊏⊐	⊏⊐	⊏⊐	⊏⊐	⊏⊐
3	⊏⊐	⊏⊐	⊏⊐	⊏⊐	⊏⊐	⊏⊐	⊏⊐	⊏⊐	⊏⊐	⊏⊐
4	⊏⊐	⊏⊐	⊏⊐	⊏⊐	⊏⊐	⊏⊐	⊏⊐	⊏⊐	⊏⊐	⊏⊐
5	⊏⊐	⊏⊐	⊏⊐	⊏⊐	⊏⊐	⊏⊐	⊏⊐	⊏⊐	⊏⊐	⊏⊐
6	⊏⊐	⊏⊐	⊏⊐	⊏⊐	⊏⊐	⊏⊐	⊏⊐	⊏⊐	⊏⊐	⊏⊐
7	⊏⊐	⊏⊐	⊏⊐	⊏⊐	⊏⊐	⊏⊐	⊏⊐	⊏⊐	⊏⊐	⊏⊐
8	⊏⊐	⊏⊐	⊏⊐	⊏⊐	⊏⊐	⊏⊐	⊏⊐	⊏⊐	⊏⊐	⊏⊐
9	⊏⊐	⊏⊐	⊏⊐	⊏⊐	⊏⊐	⊏⊐	⊏⊐	⊏⊐	⊏⊐	⊏⊐
10	⊏⊐	⊏⊐	⊏⊐	⊏⊐	⊏⊐	⊏⊐	⊏⊐	⊏⊐	⊏⊐	⊏⊐

EXERCISE 24: Answer Matching

Instructions: **Work out and match the answers to the appropriate options. Use a separate sheet for your workings.**

Maximum time allowed: 5 minutes

ANSWERS:

A	49	B	81	C	12	D	750	E	20
F	32	G	183	H	13	I	75	J	180

QUESTIONS:

1	What is the next number in the sequence below? 1, 2, 3, 5, 8
2	What is the square number after 36?
3	What is the 4th multiple of the number 8?
4	What is $11.85 + 2.15 - 2.0$?
5	A map is drawn to a scale of 1 cm = 9 km. How many kilometres does a distance of 9 cm on the map represent?
6	Pens are sold in packs of 5. A company buys 36 packs. How many pens did the company buy?
7	Decrease 100 by 25%.
8	What is $\frac{1}{8}th$ of 160?
9	What is $183 - 23 + 23$?
10	John gets 15% of the £5,000 lottery win. How much does John get?

Answer Sheet

Question Number	A	B	C	D	E	F	G	H	I	J
1	⬜	⬜	⬜	⬜	⬜	⬜	⬜	⬜	⬜	⬜
2	⬜	⬜	⬜	⬜	⬜	⬜	⬜	⬜	⬜	⬜
3	⬜	⬜	⬜	⬜	⬜	⬜	⬜	⬜	⬜	⬜
4	⬜	⬜	⬜	⬜	⬜	⬜	⬜	⬜	⬜	⬜
5	⬜	⬜	⬜	⬜	⬜	⬜	⬜	⬜	⬜	⬜
6	⬜	⬜	⬜	⬜	⬜	⬜	⬜	⬜	⬜	⬜
7	⬜	⬜	⬜	⬜	⬜	⬜	⬜	⬜	⬜	⬜
8	⬜	⬜	⬜	⬜	⬜	⬜	⬜	⬜	⬜	⬜
9	⬜	⬜	⬜	⬜	⬜	⬜	⬜	⬜	⬜	⬜
10	⬜	⬜	⬜	⬜	⬜	⬜	⬜	⬜	⬜	⬜

EXERCISE 25: Answer Matching

Instructions: Work out and match the answers to the appropriate options. Use a separate sheet for your workings.

Maximum time allowed: 5 minutes

ANSWERS:

A	14	B	7	C	15	D	10	E	60
F	80	G	5	H	100	I	17	J	21

QUESTIONS:

1	What number must be added to 20 to make it 100?
2	A drink is made by mixing 300 ml of orange juice with 500 ml of lemonade. How many litres of lemonade is required to make a drink of 8 litres?
3	A school bus can carry a maximum of 15 children. How many buses are required to carry 225 children?
4	Find $\frac{3}{7} th$ of 49?
5	What is the square number before 121?
6	The radius of a circle is 30 cm. What will be the diameter of the circle?
7	A sequence is represented by the equation **n+4.** What is the 10th term?
8	What is 50% of 20% 100?
9	What is the first prime number between 15 and 20?
10	What is the number whose 2nd multiple is 14 and 4th multiple is 28?

Answer Sheet

Question Number	A	B	C	D	E	F	G	H	I	J
1	⊡	⊡	⊡	⊡	⊡	⊡	⊡	⊡	⊡	⊡
2	⊡	⊡	⊡	⊡	⊡	⊡	⊡	⊡	⊡	⊡
3	⊡	⊡	⊡	⊡	⊡	⊡	⊡	⊡	⊡	⊡
4	⊡	⊡	⊡	⊡	⊡	⊡	⊡	⊡	⊡	⊡
5	⊡	⊡	⊡	⊡	⊡	⊡	⊡	⊡	⊡	⊡
6	⊡	⊡	⊡	⊡	⊡	⊡	⊡	⊡	⊡	⊡
7	⊡	⊡	⊡	⊡	⊡	⊡	⊡	⊡	⊡	⊡
8	⊡	⊡	⊡	⊡	⊡	⊡	⊡	⊡	⊡	⊡
9	⊡	⊡	⊡	⊡	⊡	⊡	⊡	⊡	⊡	⊡
10	⊡	⊡	⊡	⊡	⊡	⊡	⊡	⊡	⊡	⊡

EXERCISE 26: Answer Matching

Instructions: Work out and match the answers to the appropriate options. Use a separate sheet for your workings.

Maximum time allowed: 5 minutes

ANSWERS:

A	125	B	28	C	25	D	4	E	2
F	132	G	45	H	64	I	30	J	13

QUESTIONS:

1	Calculate the area of a parallelogram that has a perpendicular height of 12 cm and a base of 11 cm.
2	What is $1000 \div 8$?
3	What is the next prime number after 11?
4	What is the square root of 625?
5	What is half of a right angle?
6	Calculate $\frac{7}{25} th$ of 100?
7	What is the value of the following equation if the value of "n" is 8? $$\frac{3n}{12}$$
8	Reduce 80 by 20%.
9	The perimeter of a square is 8 cm. What will be the area of the square?
10	Find the missing number in the sequence. 0, 2, 6, 12, 20, ?, 42 Hint: The sequence is represented by the equation n^2-n

Answer Sheet

Question Number	A	B	C	D	E	F	G	H	I	J
1	⬜	⬜	⬜	⬜	⬜	⬜	⬜	⬜	⬜	⬜
2	⬜	⬜	⬜	⬜	⬜	⬜	⬜	⬜	⬜	⬜
3	⬜	⬜	⬜	⬜	⬜	⬜	⬜	⬜	⬜	⬜
4	⬜	⬜	⬜	⬜	⬜	⬜	⬜	⬜	⬜	⬜
5	⬜	⬜	⬜	⬜	⬜	⬜	⬜	⬜	⬜	⬜
6	⬜	⬜	⬜	⬜	⬜	⬜	⬜	⬜	⬜	⬜
7	⬜	⬜	⬜	⬜	⬜	⬜	⬜	⬜	⬜	⬜
8	⬜	⬜	⬜	⬜	⬜	⬜	⬜	⬜	⬜	⬜
9	⬜	⬜	⬜	⬜	⬜	⬜	⬜	⬜	⬜	⬜
10	⬜	⬜	⬜	⬜	⬜	⬜	⬜	⬜	⬜	⬜

EXERCISE 27: Answer Matching

Instructions: Work out and match the answers to the appropriate options. Use a separate sheet for your workings.

Maximum time allowed: 5 minutes

A	4	B	5	C	6	D	-14	E	56
F	28	G	-20	H	24	I	52	J	40

1	What is $\frac{1}{20}$ as a percentage?
2	What is the product of 400 and 0.1?
3	Find the value of "x". $3x^2 + 1 = 109$
4	What is $-5 - 9$?
5	Find the perimeter of the kite below where "m" is 5 cm.
6	The price of a winter jacket is £80. In a sale the price is reduced by 30%. What is the sale price of the winter jacket?
7	A drink is made by mixing 400 ml of squash with 300 ml of water. How many litres of squash is required to make a drink of 7 litres?
8	If the area of a triangle is 420 cm² and its perpendicular height is 30 cm, what is the length of its base?
9	What is the value of "n" in the equation below? $5n = -100$
10	William Shakespeare is believed to have lived between 1564 and 1616. How old was he when he died?

Answer Sheet

Question Number	A	B	C	D	E	F	G	H	I	J
1	A	B	C	D	E	F	G	H	I	J
2	A	B	C	D	E	F	G	H	I	J
3	A	B	C	D	E	F	G	H	I	J
4	A	B	C	D	E	F	G	H	I	J
5	A	B	C	D	E	F	G	H	I	J
6	A	B	C	D	E	F	G	H	I	J
7	A	B	C	D	E	F	G	H	I	J
8	A	B	C	D	E	F	G	H	I	J
9	A	B	C	D	E	F	G	H	I	J
10	A	B	C	D	E	F	G	H	I	J

Instructions: Work out and match the answers to the appropriate options. Use a separate sheet for your workings.

Maximum time allowed: 5 minutes

A	75	B	66	C	10	D	12	E	125
F	79	G	55	H	60	I	65	J	16

1	Work out 15% of 440.
2	What is the next prime number after 73?
3	Find the value of "b". $75 = 20 + b$
4	Complete the fraction. $3\dfrac{1}{3} = \dfrac{?}{3}$
5	A baking tray can hold 12 cupcakes. How many cakes will 5 trays hold?
6	A train travels 325 miles in 5 hours. What is its average speed?
7	Find the area of the rectangle below when the value of "a" is 2 cm? 3a a [rectangle diagram]
8	The two parallel sides of a rectangle is 15 cm and the distance between them is 5 cm. What is the area of this rectangle?
9	What is $\dfrac{2}{8}$ of 64 ?
10	What is $5 \times 5 \times 5$?

Answer Sheet

Question Number	A	B	C	D	E	F	G	H	I	J
1	⊏⊐	⊏⊐	⊏⊐	⊏⊐	⊏⊐	⊏⊐	⊏⊐	⊏⊐	⊏⊐	⊏⊐
2	⊏⊐	⊏⊐	⊏⊐	⊏⊐	⊏⊐	⊏⊐	⊏⊐	⊏⊐	⊏⊐	⊏⊐
3	⊏⊐	⊏⊐	⊏⊐	⊏⊐	⊏⊐	⊏⊐	⊏⊐	⊏⊐	⊏⊐	⊏⊐
4	⊏⊐	⊏⊐	⊏⊐	⊏⊐	⊏⊐	⊏⊐	⊏⊐	⊏⊐	⊏⊐	⊏⊐
5	⊏⊐	⊏⊐	⊏⊐	⊏⊐	⊏⊐	⊏⊐	⊏⊐	⊏⊐	⊏⊐	⊏⊐
6	⊏⊐	⊏⊐	⊏⊐	⊏⊐	⊏⊐	⊏⊐	⊏⊐	⊏⊐	⊏⊐	⊏⊐
7	⊏⊐	⊏⊐	⊏⊐	⊏⊐	⊏⊐	⊏⊐	⊏⊐	⊏⊐	⊏⊐	⊏⊐
8	⊏⊐	⊏⊐	⊏⊐	⊏⊐	⊏⊐	⊏⊐	⊏⊐	⊏⊐	⊏⊐	⊏⊐
9	⊏⊐	⊏⊐	⊏⊐	⊏⊐	⊏⊐	⊏⊐	⊏⊐	⊏⊐	⊏⊐	⊏⊐
10	⊏⊐	⊏⊐	⊏⊐	⊏⊐	⊏⊐	⊏⊐	⊏⊐	⊏⊐	⊏⊐	⊏⊐

EXERCISE 29: Answer Matching

Instructions: Work out and match the answers to the appropriate options. Use a separate sheet for your workings.

Maximum time allowed: 5 minutes

A	9	B	1	C	2	D	125	E	135
F	8	G	18	H	14	I	40	J	64

1	Multiplying a number by 0.4 is the same as finding what percentage?
2	Increase 32 by 200%
3	Evaluate $\sqrt{8^2}$
4	A rectangle has a perimeter of 64 cm and a length of 14 cm. Find its width.
5	The price of a box of chocolates is £4.25 How many boxes can be bought with £42
6	A recipe requires 4 eggs to make 10 cookies. How many eggs will be needed to make 35 cookies?
7	Find the value of angle "x". x $45°$
8	What is $-5 + \frac{49}{7}$?
9	How many Faces does a cone have?
10	How many 5p coins are required to make £6.25?

Answer Sheet

Question Number	A	B	C	D	E	F	G	H	I	J
1	⊟	⊟	⊟	⊟	⊟	⊟	⊟	⊟	⊟	⊟
2	⊟	⊟	⊟	⊟	⊟	⊟	⊟	⊟	⊟	⊟
3	⊟	⊟	⊟	⊟	⊟	⊟	⊟	⊟	⊟	⊟
4	⊟	⊟	⊟	⊟	⊟	⊟	⊟	⊟	⊟	⊟
5	⊟	⊟	⊟	⊟	⊟	⊟	⊟	⊟	⊟	⊟
6	⊟	⊟	⊟	⊟	⊟	⊟	⊟	⊟	⊟	⊟
7	⊟	⊟	⊟	⊟	⊟	⊟	⊟	⊟	⊟	⊟
8	⊟	⊟	⊟	⊟	⊟	⊟	⊟	⊟	⊟	⊟
9	⊟	⊟	⊟	⊟	⊟	⊟	⊟	⊟	⊟	⊟
10	⊟	⊟	⊟	⊟	⊟	⊟	⊟	⊟	⊟	⊟

EXERCISE 30: Answer Matching

Instructions: Work out and match the answers to the appropriate options. Use a separate sheet for your workings.

Maximum time allowed: 5 minutes

A	89	B	2	C	1	D	50	E	5
F	25	G	60	H	8	I	20	J	10

1	What is the next prime number after 83?
2	Evaluate $\sqrt{8^2+6^2}$
3	Calculate the percentage change for a decrease from 400 to 300.
4	Find the value of angle "m".
5	If John walks 2 miles in 30 minutes, how many miles will he walk in 75 minutes?
6	What is $20 \div 5 - 4 \div 2$?
7	What is $\frac{1}{5}$ as a percentage?
8	Evaluate 0.05×10^3
9	The perimeter of a regular shape is 64 cm with each side measuring 8 cm. How many sides does the shape have?
10	Find the missing number "n". $2\frac{1}{2} \times \frac{1}{n} = \frac{5}{2}$

Answer Sheet

Question Number	A	B	C	D	E	F	G	H	I	J
1	⊏A⊐	⊏B⊐	⊏C⊐	⊏D⊐	⊏E⊐	⊏F⊐	⊏G⊐	⊏H⊐	⊏I⊐	⊏J⊐
2	⊏A⊐	⊏B⊐	⊏C⊐	⊏D⊐	⊏E⊐	⊏F⊐	⊏G⊐	⊏H⊐	⊏I⊐	⊏J⊐
3	⊏A⊐	⊏B⊐	⊏C⊐	⊏D⊐	⊏E⊐	⊏F⊐	⊏G⊐	⊏H⊐	⊏I⊐	⊏J⊐
4	⊏A⊐	⊏B⊐	⊏C⊐	⊏D⊐	⊏E⊐	⊏F⊐	⊏G⊐	⊏H⊐	⊏I⊐	⊏J⊐
5	⊏A⊐	⊏B⊐	⊏C⊐	⊏D⊐	⊏E⊐	⊏F⊐	⊏G⊐	⊏H⊐	⊏I⊐	⊏J⊐
6	⊏A⊐	⊏B⊐	⊏C⊐	⊏D⊐	⊏E⊐	⊏F⊐	⊏G⊐	⊏H⊐	⊏I⊐	⊏J⊐
7	⊏A⊐	⊏B⊐	⊏C⊐	⊏D⊐	⊏E⊐	⊏F⊐	⊏G⊐	⊏H⊐	⊏I⊐	⊏J⊐
8	⊏A⊐	⊏B⊐	⊏C⊐	⊏D⊐	⊏E⊐	⊏F⊐	⊏G⊐	⊏H⊐	⊏I⊐	⊏J⊐
9	⊏A⊐	⊏B⊐	⊏C⊐	⊏D⊐	⊏E⊐	⊏F⊐	⊏G⊐	⊏H⊐	⊏I⊐	⊏J⊐
10	⊏A⊐	⊏B⊐	⊏C⊐	⊏D⊐	⊏E⊐	⊏F⊐	⊏G⊐	⊏H⊐	⊏I⊐	⊏J⊐

This page is intentionally left blank

ANSWERS

ashkraft
EDUCATIONAL

Check www.mastering11plus.com/answers
for updated answers for this book.

Exercise 1		Exercise 2		Exercise 3		Exercise 4	
Q. No.	Answer	Q.No.	Answer	Q.No.	Answer	Q. No.	Answer
1	F	1	C	1	A	1	B
2	D	2	C	2	E	2	D
3	C	3	D	3	A	3	E
4	A	4	C	4	E	4	C
5	B	5	E	5	F	5	B
6	C	6	B	6	A	6	E
7	B	7	F	7	E	7	E
8	C	8	C	8	C	8	C
9	F	9	B	9	D	9	C
10	A	10	A	10	E	10	B
11	D	11	A	11	D	11	C
12	B	12	D	12	B	12	C
13	B	13	D	13	D	13	D
14	C	14	A	14	C	14	B
15	E	15	B	15	D	15	D

Exercise 5		Exercise 6		Exercise 7		Exercise 8	
Q. No.	Answer	Q.No.	Answer	Q.No.	Answer	Q. No.	Answer
1	E	1	A	1	D	1	D
2	E	2	B	2	D	2	B
3	D	3	E	3	F	3	C
4	C	4	C	4	D	4	F
5	B	5	D	5	A	5	B
6	F	6	B	6	A	6	D
7	B	7	F	7	F	7	D
8	A	8	B	8	D	8	E
9	A	9	C	9	E	9	B
10	D	10	D	10	A	10	A
11	C	11	E	11	E	11	D
12	D	12	C	12	D	12	D
13	A	13	D	13	A	13	E
14	A	14	D	14	F	14	A
15	B	15	A	15	D	15	C

Exercise 9		Exercise 10		Exercise 11		Exercise 13	
Q. No.	Answer	Q.No.	Answer	Q. No.	Answer	Q. No.	Answer
1	F	1	D	1	£20,000	1	34 cm
2	A	2	F	2	£55,000	2	62 cm
3	C	3	D	3	£4,580	3	30 cm
4	A	4	C	4	£6,000	4	10 cm
5	B	5	F	5	20%	5	5 cm
6	C	6	B	Exercise 12		Exercise 14	
7	C	7	D	Q. No.	Answer	Q. No.	Answer
8	F	8	B	1	£7.59	1	17°C
9	A	9	D	2	£2.41	2	9°C
10	E	10	A	3	£1.25	3	4°C
11	A	11	D	4	£18.50	4	11°C
12	D	12	B	5	£10.69	5	3°C
13	C	13	F				
14	F	14	E				
15	D	15	E				

Exercise 15		Exercise 17		Exercise 19		Exercise 21	
Q. No.	Answer	Q. No.	Answer	Q. No.	Answer	Q. No.	Answer
1	£1,000	1	3	1	60%	1	G
2	£200	2	4	2	£15,000	2	A
3	£200,000	3	4	3	£384	3	J
4	£20,000	4	12	4	280	4	I
5	£320,000	5	9	5	£33,600	5	F
Exercise 16		Exercise 18		Exercise 20		6	B
Q. No.	Answer	Q. No.	Answer	Q. No.	Answer	7	H
1	90°	1	7	1	11	8	C
2	55°	2	7	2	17	9	E
3	35°	3	10	3	11	10	D
4	345°	4	21	4	12		
5	180°	5	49	5	3		

Exercise 22		Exercise 23		Exercise 24		Exercise 25	
Q. No.	Answer	Q.No.	Answer	Q.No.	Answer	Q. No.	Answer
1	G	1	H	1	H	1	F
2	I	2	C	2	A	2	G
3	B	3	A	3	F	3	C
4	A	4	F	4	C	4	J
5	F	5	I	5	B	5	H
6	H	6	D	6	J	6	E
7	C	7	G	7	I	7	A
8	J	8	J	8	E	8	D
9	D	9	E	9	G	9	I
10	E	10	B	10	D	10	B

Exercise 26		Exercise 27		Exercise 28		Exercise 29		Exercise 30	
Q. No.	Ans	Q. No.	Ans	Q. No.	Ans	Q. No.	Ans	Q. No.	Ans
1	F	1	B	1	B	1	I	1	A
2	A	2	J	2	F	2	J	2	J
3	J	3	C	3	G	3	F	3	F
4	C	4	D	4	C	4	G	4	G
5	G	5	H	5	H	5	A	5	E
6	B	6	E	6	I	6	H	6	B
7	E	7	A	7	D	7	E	7	I
8	H	8	F	8	A	8	C	8	D
9	D	9	G	9	J	9	B	9	H
10	I	10	I	10	E	10	D	10	C

Other books in the Mastering 11+ series:

- ➤ English & Verbal Reasoning – Practice Book 1
- ➤ English & Verbal Reasoning – Practice Book 2
- ➤ English & Verbal Reasoning – Practice Book 3

- ➤ Cloze Tests – Practice Book 1
- ➤ Cloze Tests – Practice Book 2
- ➤ Cloze Tests – Practice Book 3

- ➤ Maths / Numerical Reasoning – Practice Book 1
- ➤ Maths / Numerical Reasoning – Practice Book 3

- ➤ Comprehension – Multiple Choice Exercise Book 1
- ➤ Comprehension – Multiple Choice Exercise Book 2
- ➤ Comprehension – Multiple Choice Exercise Book 3

- ➤ CEM Practice Papers – Pack 1
- ➤ CEM Practice Papers – Pack 2
- ➤ CEM Practice Papers – Pack 3
- ➤ CEM Practice Papers – Pack 4

All queries via email to enquiry@mastering11plus.com

Mastering11plus.com © 2016, ashkraft educational

Printed in Poland
by Amazon Fulfillment
Poland Sp. z o.o., Wrocław